A 40-Day Journey of Prayer for Your Marriage

Dr. Timothy Heck

Leitourgia Press
Indianapolis, Indiana

Copyright © 2019 by Timothy Heck.

All rights reserved. No part of this publication may be reproduced, distributed or transmitted in any form or by any means, including photocopying, recording, or other electronic or mechanical methods, without the prior written permission of the publisher, except in the case of brief quotations embodied in critical reviews and certain other noncommercial uses permitted by copyright law. For permission requests, write to the publisher, addressed "Attention: Permissions Coordinator," at the address below.

Timothy Heck/Leitourgia Press
P.O. Box 503464
Indianapolis, IN/46250
www.leitourgiapress.org

Book Layout ©2017 BookDesignTemplates.com

THE HOLY BIBLE, NEW INTERNATIONAL VERSION®, NIV® Copyright © 1973, 1978, 1984, 2011 by Biblica, Inc.™ Used by permission. All rights reserved worldwide.

Ordering Information:
Quantity sales. Special discounts are available on quantity purchases by corporations, associations, and others. For details, contact Leitourgia Press at the address above or email: info@leitourgiapress.org.

Praying for Your Marriage/ Timothy Heck. —1st ed.
ISBN 978-0-578-50885-6
Library of Congress Control Number: 2019942142

Contents

All We Are Is Yours 9
   Day 1 Reflection 10

Heal Our Past Hurts 11
   Day 2 Reflection 12

Teach Us to Forgive 13
   Day 3 Reflection 14

Fighting Fairly 15
   Day 4 Reflection 16

Making Decisions 17
   Day 5 Reflection 18

We Need A Renewed Vision 19
   Day 6 Reflection 20

Create In Us A Clean Heart 21
   Day 7 Reflection 22

Delight In Each Other 23
   Day 8 Reflection 24

Humble Yourselves 25
   Day 9 Reflection 26

An Attitude of Contentment 27
   Day 10 Reflection 28

To Love Sacrificially 30
  Day 11 Reflection 31

Guard Our Family 32
  Day 12 Reflection 33

Secure Our Trust 34
  Day 13 Reflection 35

Friends Are Friends Forever 36
  Day 14 Reflection 37

Lovers Forever 38
  Day 15 Reflection 39

Our Extended Family 40
  Day 16 Reflection 41

Increase Our Faith 42
  Day 17 Reflection 43

Good Grief 44
  Day 18 Reflection 45

One In Spirit and Body 46
  Day 19 Reflection 47

Sacrificial Giving 48
  Day 20 Reflection 49

Reset Our Priorities 50
  Day 21 Reflection 51

Bless Our Stress 52
    Day 22 Reflection 53

Sweeten Our Tongues 54
    Day 23 Reflection 55

Humble Us 56
    Day 24 Reflection 57

A Heart for Repair 58
    Day 25 Reflection 59

In Good Health 60
    Day 26 Reflection 61

Bless Our Home 62
    Day 27 Reflection 63

Our Marriage—A Mission 64
    Day 28 Reflection 65

A Light for the Community 66
    Day 29 Reflection 67

Renew Our First Love 68
    Day 30 Reflection 69

Appetites for You 70
    Day 31 Reflection 71

Good Friends 72
    Day 32 Reflection 73

Jobs and Vocations 74
    Day 33 Reflection 75

Determined and Active 76
    Day 34 Reflection 77

Free to Choose 78
    Day 35 Reflection 79

Grace to Accept 80
    Day 36 Reflection 81

Thank You 82
    Day 37 Reflection 83

Teach Us to Love More 84
    Day 38 Reflection 85

Forgive Us, Lord! 86
    Day 39 Reflection 87

Your Will Be Done! 88
    Day 40 Reflection 89

Self-Dedication to Jesus Christ 90
Dr. Timothy Heck 92

A 40-DAY JOURNEY OF PRAYER FOR YOUR MARRIAGE

Dedicated to my precious grandchildren, whose innocence echoes the courts of heaven. Grow to be all your Creator God has meant for you and stay close to him in prayer always!

"Devote yourselves to prayer. Be alert and thankful when you pray."

—Colossians 4:2

As you prepare to go through this 40-Day Journey, let me offer a few guidelines to help make the process more amenable to your personality, schedule and overall routine.

- Ask your spouse to pray these prayers with you, but if unwilling after a gentle invitation, just let them know you will be praying them each day and you would welcome their involvement any time.
- Choose the time of day that best suits your schedule, mood and energy level, to give you optimum success in completing the journey each day.
- The prayers can be prayed in any order, so if you prefer to skip around, that's totally up to you. My only recommendation would be that you check off the prayer in the table of contents so that you don't repeat some and miss others.
- Place this book in a location in your house where you experience more of a peaceful sense of God's presence.

There you go. You're all set to begin the journey. May the Lord bless you as you offer these prayers for you, your spouse and your relationship.

I know what you're thinking—what can really happen in just forty short days? Good question! Because the truth is that the Bible is replete with stories about some unbelievable and amazing experiences happening over a 40-day period. Consider a few of them.

- The world was virtually destroyed by a flood from 40 days and 40 nights of rain.
- Moses spent 40 years in the wilderness of Midian after killing an Egyptian and was transformed into an incredible leader who would bring the Israelites out of their bondage to a new Promised Land.
- The Hebrew spies took 40 days to search out the new land of Canaan that would become the nation of Israel.
- Those same Israelites wandered 40 years in the desert before they could be ready to enter that land.
- Goliath taunted Saul's army for 40 days before David arrived to save the day.
- Jesus was tempted for 40 days and nights as he prepared to enter his High Priestly ministry for our salvation.
- And there were 40 days between Jesus' resurrection and his ascension into heaven, where he sits at God's right hand, interceding on our behalf.

So, don't be surprised if your life is changed over the coming 40 days!

A 40-DAY JOURNEY OF PRAYER FOR YOUR MARRIAGE

Prayer for Day 1

All We Are Is Yours

Father,

As we begin this journey of prayer for our marriage, we re-dedicate ourselves fully to you, who created us and gave to us this gift of love that brought us together. At the outset of these 40 days, we remind ourselves that this is not my marriage or my partner's marriage, but your marriage. Lord, we invite you to enter into our lives. Renew our first love for you and out of that love let us rediscover our love for each other.

Through Jesus, the source of true love,
Amen!

> *"You have been set apart to the Lord today...and he has blessed you this day."* Exodus 32:29

Day 1 Reflection

Circle any of the areas that you resist turning over to God in your marriage.

Finances	Children	Job	Friends
Attitude	Home	Sexual Intimacy	
Decisions	Health	Family of Origin	
Conflict	Emotions	Moods	
Past Hurts	Future	Dreams	

Other _____

Other _____

Other _____

Heal Our Past Hurts

Father,

In our time of living together as a couple we have both hurt each other. Some of these hurts are known to us and others are hidden within our hearts. We ask for the courage to share openly with each other those wounds that still cause us pain. You are the source of all true healing. The Word tells us one of your names is **Rapha**, the one who heals. So, we pray for your healing and for the grace to be forgiving.

Through Jesus, who took our hurts upon him,
Amen!

> *"Pray for each other so that you may be healed."* James 5:16

Day 2 Reflection

Open your mind to the past and ask God to show you where you may still be harboring pain, resentment and bitterness toward your partner for ways he/she has hurt you. Prayerfully consider opening up with your spouse about these wounds in order to find understanding, sympathy and forgiveness.

His	Hers
_____	_____
_____	_____
_____	_____
_____	_____
_____	_____
_____	_____
_____	_____
_____	_____
_____	_____
_____	_____
_____	_____
_____	_____
_____	_____

Prayer for Day 3

Teach Us to Forgive

Father,

We are not perfect and have failed each other in many ways. It is difficult for us to let go of the urge to punish or remind my spouse of the times and ways he/she has offended me. Teach us to give the precious gift of forgiveness in our marriage. When our pride gets in the way, take us to the cross of Jesus where we can hear the words of our Lord, who said of those who rejected, ridiculed and crucified him, ***"Father, forgive them!"***

Through Jesus, the source of all grace,
Amen!

> *"But if you do not forgive others their sins, your Father will not forgive your sins."* Matthew 6:15

Day 3 Reflection

Ask your wife or husband to share anything from yesterday's reflection list and ask for their forgiveness. Then share anything from your list and offer those words to your spouse, *"I forgive you!"*

Prayer for Day 4

Fighting Fairly

Father,

Conflict is part of any relationship, but sometimes we either avoid having the important conversation or we get into unfair fights. Our desire is to work through our issues without causing harm to each other or our relationship. Whether we are afraid of conflict or fail to control ourselves in the midst of an argument, we ask you to draw out of us the skills, patience and virtues to work on the issues fairly and respectfully.

Through Jesus, who reconciled us to you,
Amen!

> *"If it is possible, as far as it depends on you, live at peace..."* Romans 12:18

Day 4 Reflection

Think about how your parents argued in their relationship. Which of the following styles for working through problems characterizes you in your marriage?

- ☐ **Withdraw** – I tend to withdraw from difficult conversations when I think it might turn into an argument.
- ☐ **Yield** – I tend to give into my spouse to avoid having the conversation escalate into something hurtful and negative.
- ☐ **Win** – I tend to press my partner to agree with me or at least talk through the issues in our relationship and I will press harder if he/she withdraws.
- ☐ **Compromise** – I tend to want to meet my spouse halfway and try to reach solutions where we each get some of what we want.
- ☐ **Resolve** – I tend to want to talk through every aspect of an issue with my spouse so we can both fully understand the other's perspective and reach a decision we both find good.

Are these effective styles in your marriage? Perhaps you could discuss how you tend to react to conflict.

A 40-DAY JOURNEY OF PRAYER FOR YOUR MARRIAGE

PRAYER FOR DAY 5

Making Decisions

Father,

Every day we face many decisions, some small and some serious. We both want to make decisions that are godly, wise and practical. When we can't agree on a decision, help us to work harder to understand why our partner made the choice he/she did. When we struggle to make a decision, give us the wisdom to know what is best and the openness to work together. In those times of confusion, we ask your Holy Spirit to enlighten us to what we need most.

Through Him whose decisions are always for our best, Amen!

> *"Decide to live in such a way that you will not cause each other to stumble and fall."* Romans 14:13

Day 5 Reflection

Write down a problem or issue you are currently dealing with that requires a decision. Spend a few minutes discussing it with your spouse and see if you can arrive at a mutually acceptable decision.

_____

_____

_____

_____

_____

_____

_____

_____

_____

PRAYER FOR DAY **6**

We Need A Renewed Vision

Father,

Our time living together in marriage has affected our vision. Frequently, we can only see the faults and negative features of our partner's personality. We need to have our eyesight renewed so we can again overlook those less attractive traits and see the beauty of who you created our spouse to be. We ask for a godly view of our spouse and our relationship. We pray to receive your eyes, your vision and your perspective.

Through Jesus, who knows us best and loves us most, Amen!

> *"So from now on we regard no one from a worldly point of view."* 2 Corinthians 5:16

Day 6 Reflection

Take a moment to think about one of your spouse's traits you find most irritating. Now ask God to show you a positive expression of that trait. For instance, if your partner is a perfectionist, he/she may be critical at times, but also very thorough.

Her Negative Trait:

_____

A Positive Expression of Her Trait:

_____

His Negative Trait:

_____

A Positive Expression of His Trait:

_____

A 40-DAY JOURNEY OF PRAYER FOR YOUR MARRIAGE

PRAYER FOR DAY 7

Create In Us A Clean Heart

Father,

We are bombarded with images that distort and twist the purity you want us to have in our lives. Reset our moral compasses so that we can discern temptation when it tries to invade our lives. Restore the clean heart you gave us when you created us in your image. Increase our appetite for the good, the noble, the pure and the chaste. Remove the disordered appetites for the immoral, the pornographic and the evil so present in our world.

Through Jesus, who was tempted in all things as are we, but remained sinless,
Amen!

> *"Let us purify ourselves from everything that contaminates body and spirit, perfecting holiness out of reverence for God."* 2 Corinthians 7:1

Day 7 Reflection

Where does temptation to be impure and unchaste come from in your life?

Television
Movies
Books
Memories
News
Friends
Magazines
Social Media
Advertisements
Fantasies
Lusting and objectifying others

_____
_____
_____
_____

Now, commit to praying regularly for your own and your spouse's areas of temptation that he/she may be strengthened to withstand any temptation that could find its way into our mind, heart, soul and body.

Prayer for Day 8

Delight In Each Other

Father,

Sometimes we just take life too seriously and forget to laugh, have fun and enjoy each other. Remind us of our special times together in the past. Help us to recall the personal experiences of joy in our marriage. Save us from monotonous boredom so that we can again find delight in who we are as a couple. I want to see my spouse as you see her/him. Bring spontaneous pleasure into our days and begin with me!

Through Jesus, who chose us out of his delight in us, Amen!

> *"Like an apple tree among the trees of the forest is my beloved."* Song of Solomon 2:3

Day 8 Reflection

Pick at least one of the following to do today.

1. Recall a funny story from your marriage in the past and tell it to your spouse with all the humorous details.
2. Google some jokes or funny quips about marriage and share a few of them with your spouse.
3. Look up some old(er) pictures of you and your spouse that depict the two of you having fun together. Look at them and remind each other about the details of when the picture was taken.

Prayer for Day 9

Humble Yourselves

Father,

It is so easy for me to think my opinion is the right one, to put my desires above my wife's/husband's, and to push for my way, instead of our way. When my pride increases, replace it with a spirit of humility. Show me always the way of servanthood so that I might serve my partner and pursue all that is good for the both of us, and not just one of us. Please also enable me to be gentle and make it easier for my spouse to be humble with me.

Through Jesus, who humbled himself to the point of death,
Amen!

> *"God opposes the proud but shows favor to the humble."* James 4:6

Day 9 Reflection

Take five minutes out of your day today and ask God to show you where pride has crept into your relationship. Often false pride is about protection and our need to guard ourselves from something. Ask Him in prayer to reveal what you are afraid of discovering about yourself. Jot down any insights here and tell them to your partner, even if you feel fearful of doing so. Start by telling her/him what you are afraid might happen if you reveal these things about yourself.

His	Hers

A 40-DAY JOURNEY OF PRAYER FOR YOUR MARRIAGE

PRAYER FOR DAY 10

An Attitude of Contentment

Father,

We live in a society that is so materialistic. It tempts us to never be satisfied with what we have. Enough never seems to be enough. Yet, when we consider all that we have, it is so clear that you have blessed us, provided for us, and given us much more than we need. Keep us from selfishness. Take away this hunger within us that wants more stuff. We pray for an attitude of contentment and we thank you for what we have.

Through Jesus, who meets our deepest needs,
Amen!

"Be content with what you have..." Hebrews 13:5

Day 10 Reflection

STEP ONE:

This may be easier than you think. Set the timer on your phone or watch for just five minutes. After you push "Start", take turns naming things you have or own. Do it quickly. Maybe walk around your home and notice the stuff as you do this. It may surprise you how much you have.

STEP TWO:

After completing step one, try this exercise from a popular home organizer, but modify it slightly. Take turns with this and it will be harder than you think. For example, take all of your clothes and pile them on your bed. That's right! All of them. Then step back and look at the pile. Ask yourself a few questions.

- ✓ How does it feel to know that I have all these clothes and to know that there are many who have so little?
- ✓ Do I really need all these clothes?
- ✓ Am I willing to let go of some of the clothes I don't need?

STEP THREE:

Finally, hold each article of clothing and thank God for the benefit it has given you. If you feel convicted to do so, put the things you no longer need into a pile to donate to your local charity for those in need.

A 40-DAY JOURNEY OF PRAYER FOR YOUR MARRIAGE

Now move on to another category and go through the process all over again.

> Toys
> Hobbies
> Collections
> Sporting Equipment
> Tools

_____

_____

_____

_____

_____

_____

A 40-DAY JOURNEY OF PRAYER FOR YOUR MARRIAGE

Prayer for Day 11

To Love Sacrificially

Father,

We are so accustomed to looking out for our own good and paying too little attention to the needs of our spouse. Your son not only taught us how to live sacrificially, he modeled it throughout his life and in his death. It will require us to live in your grace if we are to love in the other-centered way necessary to overcome the urge to be self-centered. So, we ask you for this grace. It will be enough!

Through Jesus, who sacrificed himself for us,
Amen!

"Love one another. As I have loved you, so you must love one another." John 13:34

Day 11 Reflection

We have all read books, heard stories and watched movies about people who sacrificed themselves for a greater cause, whether it be a nation, a friend or a lover. Consider, how far would you go to show your love for your spouse? Would you give your life for him/her? I'm not talking about death, but a sacrificial life of love. Would you dare to love this much? Imagine what that would mean for your marriage. Think about the difference that kind of love would make in your relationship.

A 40-DAY JOURNEY OF PRAYER FOR YOUR MARRIAGE

Prayer for Day 12

Guard Our Family

Father,

This world is not our home, at least, not for long and not for eternity. Remind us of this truth and keep us forever mindful of the battle that is taking place for our souls. Guard our souls and the souls of our entire family, protecting us from the threats and assaults of the evil one who seeks to rob, steal and destroy us. As Joshua declared, so do I—as for me and my house, we will serve the Lord!

Through Jesus, our protector and guardian,
Amen!

> *"But the Lord is faithful, and he will strengthen you and protect you from the evil one."* 2 Thessalonians 3:3

Day 12 Reflection

What threatens your marriage? If you believe that we are truly at war with evil, then you should take it upon yourself to know the source of your enemy's weapons and attacks. Give some thought to how your enemy, the devil, tries to destroy your marriage. Does he use money? Lust? Ego? Reputation? Fame? Pleasure? Arguments? Anger? Alcohol? Drugs? Or something else?

_____

_____

_____

_____

_____

_____

_____

Prayer for Day 13

Secure Our Trust

Father,

Our relationship began with small steps of trust that built a foundation of security for us. Over the years we have both said and done things that have threatened that core trust. We ask that you draw our focus upon you, the source of our true and lasting security. Relying on your trustworthiness as our Lord, empower us to again risk trusting each other and restore our own trustworthiness as spouses.

Through Jesus, who secured our eternal trust, we trust in you,
Amen!

"Trust in the Lord forever." Isaiah 26:4

Day 13 Reflection

Ask God to show you some of the key ways your spouse has earned your trust over the years. When a marriage is struggling it is easy for both partners to focus on the negative experiences of the past that have injured or even broken trust. But, in this exercise we want you to recall the *stones* that were laid in the early foundation years of your story as a couple. Jot some down here and then talk about them together. Shore up the foundation of your marriage and never forget—Jesus is the Cornerstone!

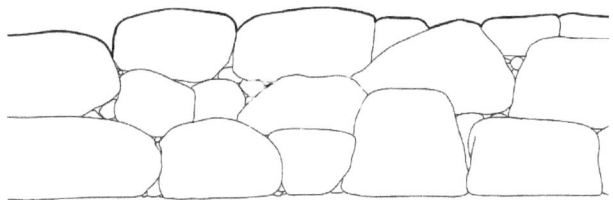

A 40-DAY JOURNEY OF PRAYER FOR YOUR MARRIAGE

PRAYER FOR DAY 14

Friends Are Friends Forever

Father,

We treasure our friendship, but we are not always friendly with each other. Sometimes we treat strangers with more kindness. Restore our companionship, our partnership, our friendship. You blessed us with this gift of friendship the day we said, *"I do"*. Forgive the way we have taken advantage of the gift of our friendship and make us better friends than ever from this day forward.

Through Jesus, who said, *"You are my friends, not servants"*,
Amen!

"You are my friends." John 15:14

Day 14 Reflection

Do you remember some of the things you used to do early in your marriage or even when you were dating? Put on some of your *Oldies* music and let it take you back to those days. Talk about what you remember and how you spent your time. When you do, you'll likely be calling back memories of friendship.

Prayer for Day 15

Lovers Forever

Father,

Sex has become such a misunderstood, confusing and controversial word, but we know it was part of our design as your creation. It means more than just what happens between the sheets of our bed in the privacy of our home. It is lifegiving. We cherish our sexual intimacy. Prevent us from falling for the false claims and empty meanings attached to sex in our culture. We want to pursue mutuality in all areas of our marriage, especially this most intimate of all.

Through Jesus, the Son and our Creator,
Amen!

"I am my lover's...my lover is mine." Song of Sol. 6:3

Day 15 Reflection

It has been observed that affection is to a woman what sex is to a man. Perhaps too general a statement to apply across the board, but it generally holds true. The truth is—the best sexual intimacy will occur within a context of affection. With that in mind, plan a date with your spouse. Surprise him/her. Take care of all the details and plan for an evening of love.

A 40-DAY JOURNEY OF PRAYER FOR YOUR MARRIAGE

Prayer for Day 16

Our Extended Family

Father,

Sometimes we struggle to relate to our spouse's family and even our own extended family. We offer prayer for our parents, our siblings, their marriages and families, and all of our relatives. Give us a patient understanding and a spirit of acceptance, especially for the ones who are the source of such irritation and even pain. And help us to be good extended family to all of them.

Through Jesus, who showed us how to live in a family, Amen!

"I bow my knees before the Father, from whom every family derives its name." Ephesians 3:15

Day 16 Reflection

Write down the names of the extended family on both sides, yours and your spouse's. As you do so, ask God to bless that person in the way most needed. If you run into a name for whom you find it difficult to pray that prayer of blessing, you might ask God to give you a spirit of grace to forgive him/her for whatever offense you have experienced from that individual. Remember, each one is a piece of the puzzle of your marriage.

A 40-DAY JOURNEY OF PRAYER FOR YOUR MARRIAGE

Prayer for Day 17

Increase Our Faith

Father,

Since faith is so difficult to measure, we ask that we not be judgmental about where we are in matters of faith. Only inspire us to practice our faith, live out our devotion to you, our God, and to walk as members of the Body of Christ. Make of our marriage a joint effort to encourage each the other in this pilgrimage toward our ultimate and everlasting home with you in heaven.

Through Jesus, the focus of our faith,
Amen!

"So those who rely on faith are blessed." Galatians 3:9

A 40-DAY JOURNEY OF PRAYER FOR YOUR MARRIAGE

Day 17 Reflection

I'm a firm believer in the power of a story. Each of us has one. With faith, we can begin to see how that story has been interwoven with God's story. Take a few minutes to talk about these three questions.

How did you first come to have faith in God?

How has your faith changed over the years?

How can I help you continue to grow in your faith?

Prayer for Day 18

Good Grief

Father,

Life gives all of us its share of sorrows, especially when we think about our loved ones who are no longer with us. We miss them, especially **(Mention the names of your own loved ones)** and long to be re-united with them one day in your presence. Until then, be a refuge for us in our times of sadness and grief. We embrace the words of Paul when he admonished us, **"Do not grieve as those who have no hope"**.

Through Jesus and with the Holy Spirit, our Comforter,
Amen!

"Do not grieve as those who have no hope." 1 Thess.4:13

Day 18 Reflection

Think of some of your close loved ones who have died. Now let your mind drift back to some favorite memories with that person. Just remember and soak up the memory!

Prayer for Day 19

One In Spirit and Body

Father,

Our lives take us in many directions and not always together. The demands and stressors have a tendency to pull us apart, when we know that you gave us our relationship to be a support for us in this pilgrimage. Make us one in spirit and body, bonding us together emotionally so that our intimacy extends into all areas of our lives.

Through Jesus, who makes us one,
Amen!

> *"Since we live by the Spirit, let us keep in step with the Spirit."* Galatians 5:25

Day 19 Reflection

Plan some more regular times to ***intersect*** your lives as a couple. Here are a few examples but come up with your own that fit your routine, schedule and life rhythm.

- Meet for lunch one day a week
- Have breakfast out, just the two of you, once a month
- Get a new Journal and make it a ***Marriage Journal*** for you both to share your thoughts, feelings, concerns and questions with each other.
- Have a phone date once a week to just catch up, like you used to when you were dating.
- Take a walk together
- Write each other an old-fashioned letter...the kind with a piece of paper and pen

Prayer for Day 20

Sacrificial Giving

Father,

We work hard for our income and try to spend it wisely. It is difficult to give our hard-earned money away, whether to your Church, mission organizations, or the beggar on the street. Open our hearts to see the needs you want us to enter into and respond to with generosity. We pray for discernment to use our finances wisely, but also for a sacrificial heart to say "Yes" to those in need of our help.

Through Jesus, who sacrificed everything for us, Amen!

"Be generous and willing to share." 1 Timothy 6:18

A 40-DAY JOURNEY OF PRAYER FOR YOUR MARRIAGE

Day 20 Reflection

Is God pleased with your level of generosity?

Prayer for Day 21

Reset Our Priorities

Father,

Staying on course with our priorities and values requires us to regularly evaluate, not only what we are doing, but why we are doing it. In a world whose priorities are prone to be self-directed and not consistent with how you have called us to live, we ask that you reset our priorities and recalibrate our values. Show us what should be first in our lives and keep us directed toward what really counts.

Through Jesus, who made us His priority,
Amen!

> *"I press on toward the goal...for which God has called me heavenward in Christ Jesus."* Philippians 3:14

Day 21 Reflection

So, what are your priorities in life? Two simple ways to determine your priorities are to examine your Check/Credit Card Register and your Calendar. The two metrics will reveal what is important to you. How you spend your money and your time—the fastest and most reliable way to determine what your priorities are for your life.

Prayer for Day 22

Bless Our Stress

Father,

Our lives are burdened by stress. It comes from the demands on our time, our finances, our resources, and our energy. From cell phones to computers to email and so much more, we long for peace. Knowing the stress will not go away, we offer it up to you and ask that you give it your blessing. Convert the demands into opportunities to give you glory as we exercise our faith.

Through Jesus, the Prince of Peace,
Amen!

> *"Wonderful Counselor, Mighty God, Everlasting Father, Prince of Peace."* Isaiah 9:6

Day 22 Reflection

Step 1: This should be easy. As quickly as you can, list the source of stress in your lives right now. Put a word or short phrase that will represent the source (E.g. money, health, job, etc.).

Step 2: Now go back and consider how God could use the source of the stress for his glory (E.g. Develop a virtue, learn to trust, etc.).

Stressor_____

Opportunity_____

Stressor_____

Opportunity_____

Stressor_____

Opportunity_____

Stressor_____

Opportunity_____

PRAYER FOR DAY 23

Sweeten Our Tongues

Father,

When we argue it can get hurtful. We sometimes say things we don't mean, get upset and lash out, criticize, get defensive, contemptuous or shut down and withdraw from each other. We need a freshness in our speech. Sweeten our tongues so that we are again kindhearted, gentle, accepting of our failings and eager to repair when breakdowns occur.

Through Jesus, our Ambassador of Reconciliation, Amen!

> *"All this is from God, who reconciled us to himself through Christ and gave us the ministry of reconciliation."* 2 Corinthians 5:18

Day 23 Reflection

Write your spouse a brief caring note, expressing your appreciation for him/her.

Prayer for Day 24

Humble Us

Father,

Pride rises up in us from time to time and we shut down, refusing to let our spouse influence our way of thinking or our decision-making. This usually causes more problems between us and almost never turns out well in the end. Pry open our spirits and fill them with your Holy Spirit to keep us humble and receptive to each other. Prevent closed-mindedness and hardness of heart to settle into our marriage.

Through Jesus, who humbled himself for our sake, Amen!

"Clothe yourselves with humility toward one another."
1 Peter 5:5

A 40-DAY JOURNEY OF PRAYER FOR YOUR MARRIAGE

Day 24 Reflection

Recall your last argument with your spouse. Were you open to their influence? Did you let them change your mind or at least give consideration to their perspective? If so, good for you. If not, review what your spouse had to say and try going back to the conversation with a willingness to look at it from *all* sides.

Prayer for Day 25

A Heart for Repair

Father,

Conflict is normal in marriage, but we don't want it to break us apart and injure our love. When we have hurt each other, whether intentionally or out of uncontrolled anger, we ask for your heart of reconciliation that will move us to repair quickly, sincerely and wholeheartedly. Soften and soothe us in order that our oneness can be fully restored when threatened by negativity and hurt.

Through Jesus, the giver of all grace,
Amen!

> *"Leave your gift there in front of the altar. First go and be reconciled to that person."* Matthew 5:24

A 40-DAY JOURNEY OF PRAYER FOR YOUR MARRIAGE

Day 25 Reflection

Think back on your marriage. Are there some memories of hurts that have not been effectively repaired? Do you still harbor resentment toward your spouse for things he/she has said or done? Do you recall times where you hurt your spouse and never made it right, taking responsibility for your actions and seeking their forgiveness to repair your relationship? If there are such times that come to your mind, find the courage in God to go to your partner as quickly as you can to affect that repair and experience that peace in your relationship.

Prayer for Day 26

In Good Health

Father,

With each passing year we can tell our bodies are aging. Health is a gift we never want to take for granted. We rededicate ourselves to self-care by eating balanced foods, exercising regularly, working in periods of intentional rest and recovery, and keeping a positive mental attitude. Thank you for modern medicine that affords us the means to maintain our good health, but we also thank you for giving us the grace to age with acceptance of our limitations.

Through Jesus, who provided for our eternal bodies, Amen!

> *"I pray that you may enjoy good health and that all may go well with you."* 3 John 1:2

Day 26 Reflection

What area(s) do you need to make some changes for improvement to your own health? Talk as a couple about how you could implement some changes for the benefit of your health.

Eating Habits

Exercise

Recreation

Rest

Positive Mental Attitude

Prayer for Day 27

Bless Our Home

Father,

Our house is a refuge for us, a place where we can just be ourselves. We ask for a spirit of contentment, pleasure and joy to be able to live comfortably, without envying the material goods of our neighbors. Enter into our home and be the welcome guest to every conversation, meal and experience of our lives. Guard our sleep, protect us and keep your watchful eye on our dwelling.

Through Jesus, who is preparing our eternal home, Amen!

> *"They broke bread in their homes and ate together with glad and sincere hearts."* Acts 2:46

Day 27 Reflection

Take a slow walk around your home. Enter into each room. Look around and take it all in, not with a critical eye, but a grateful one. Thank God for what you see and the meaning within each piece of furniture, each wall hanging, even the walls that contain the memories of your life together.

Prayer for Day 28

Our Marriage—A Mission

Father,

We know our lives here on earth are ever so brief and that the real life is yet to come in eternity. While we are here in these *clay vessels* give us a mission to accomplish. Jobs, careers, cars, houses, yards, vacations...these are all good. But we ask for more. We ask you to make us clearly aware of your calling on our lives, on our marriage. We want to make a difference for eternity and give you glory in the process.

Through Jesus, who gives purpose to our lives,
Amen!

> *"I want to carry out the mission I received from the Lord Jesus."* Acts 20:24

Day 28 Reflection

If you are looking for a job and writing your resume, the first step is to identify your key objective. That is your occupational mission. If you are starting a business, the first step is to identify the mission of your company. Should we do any less when it comes to our eternal lives? Take some time to contemplate on the purpose and mission of your marriage. Who are you as a couple and what are you trying to accomplish for God's eternal ends and for his glory?

A 40-DAY JOURNEY OF PRAYER FOR YOUR MARRIAGE

Prayer for Day 29

A Light for the Community

Father,

The world is changing rapidly and not always for good, especially for those who want to follow your truths and live according to your design for marriage and family. This is our desire, to be a model for our community as we allow your Divine light to shine through us. Let the holy flame of your Spirit in our marriage burn brightly, never to be extinguished by a dark culture or the influence of a world turning against you.

Through Jesus, who gave us the eternal light,
Amen!

"You are the light of the world." Matthew 5:14

Day 29 Reflection

Here are a few ideas for how you might brighten the light of your marriage, not to draw attention to yourselves, rather to focus that light on the true Light, Jesus Christ.

- ✓ Leave a small planter of flowers on your neighbor's doorstep without a note.
- ✓ Take some freshly baked cookies to a friend.
- ✓ Stop by at an Assisted Living Facility near your house and just have a conversation with someone in the lobby.
- ✓ Smile at the person checking you out with your groceries.
- ✓ Write a short note to a friend you haven't seen in a while and put it in the mail...yes, the actual mailbox.
- ✓ Take a walk in your neighborhood and wave to people who pass by or say "Hi" to any neighbors out.
- ✓ Look over your yard and spruce it up a bit. Make it a nice view for your neighbors to look at.

Prayer for Day 30

Renew Our First Love

Father,

Time has changed us in many ways. It has also changed the way we demonstrate our love for each other. Most days we take that love for granted, presuming our marriage is fine and not giving it much thought. We want the fire of our love that burned brightly in those early days to burn again. Inflame our passion to be different than the rest of the world. We choose to love each other with the love you gave us when we first experienced it!

Through Jesus, the lover of our souls,
Amen!

> *"You have left your first love...repent and perform the deeds you did at first."* Revelation 2:4-5

Day 30 Reflection

Take five minutes to daydream. Close your eyes and let yourself float back to those early days of your relationship with your spouse, when you couldn't wait to see each other and never wanted the day to end. Remember the things you used to do, the way you talked, the experiences you shared. Now, jot down some of those old practices here. And then... *"perform the deeds you did at first."* And keep in mind a tested-and-found-true principle: **Feelings are usually the last thing to change! Start with your attitude and your behavior.**

A 40-DAY JOURNEY OF PRAYER FOR YOUR MARRIAGE

Prayer for Day 31

Appetites for You

Father,

Our hearts are hungry, but we too often satisfy them with the artificial food of this world that leaves us always hungering for more and sometimes unhealthy. Give us appetites for you, for your Word and for time to worship you. Make us thirsty for you, Lord Jesus. In a world full of so many options, draw our focus to the most super-***natural*** tastes of all.

Through Jesus, the bread of life,
Amen!

> ***"Whoever comes to me will never go hungry...never be thirsty."*** John 6:35

Day 31 Reflection

Decide today on just one simple change you could make in your routine, that you could do daily, that if you did it regularly, it would make a difference in your spiritual health.

Examples:

- ☐ Read a verse out of the Bible every morning
- ☐ Pray in the shower
- ☐ Thank God for three things in your life
- ☐ Do a brief Examination of Conscience before going to bed and ask forgiveness for those times where you failed to honor him

_____

_____

_____

_____

_____

A 40-DAY JOURNEY OF PRAYER FOR YOUR MARRIAGE

PRAYER FOR DAY 32

Good Friends

Father,

No one is meant to live in isolation. We need friends for support, for pleasure and for companionship as a couple. Our marriage will be strengthened by having godly couples who encourage us, even as we encourage them. Give us sensitivity and discernment to enhance our current friendships as we love in the way you taught us and demonstrated for us in the sacrifice of your Son.

Through Jesus, our best friend,
Amen!

> *"Do not forsake your friend or a friend of your family."*
> Proverbs 27:10

Day 32 Reflection

Jot down the names of your couple friends. Then go back and give some thought to which of these couples could become better friends. Brainstorm some ideas and decide together on some next steps to deepen those chosen relationships.

Prayer for Day 33

Jobs and Vocations

Father,

    The work we do occupies much of our time and energy. It is tempting to confuse our vocation with our careers. Clear the confusion that distorts our true purpose as a couple. Our marriage is the true vocation we are called to fulfill. May we do so with sincerity, giving you the glory due your name and may that name that is above all names bring us to our knees in humble praise.

Through Jesus, the object of our lives,
Amen!

> ***"Whatever you do, work at it with all your heart, as working for the Lord."*** Colossians 3:23

Day 33 Reflection

Take a few moments to think about these questions concerning your job, whether it be in or out of the home.

- Would it change the way you do your work if you had a weekly report meeting with Jesus Christ?

- If Jesus were to give you a Performance Review, what would he ask you to improve in your work so that he would be more honored?

Prayer for Day 34

Determined and Active

Father,

You have designed us in your image, according to your likeness. Not only does that equip us to worship you, it instills within us a drive to be active and creative. You don't tell us exactly what endeavors we should undertake, but you do want us to do everything for your glory. We ask for the determination to stay on task, actively pursue what is good, and glorify you in the process.

Through Jesus, the Word who brought life,
Amen!

> *"Whatever you do, do it all for the glory of God."* 1 Corinthians 10:31

Day 34 Reflection

What creative activities have been part of your life? Reflect on how the work of your hands has given God glory, that is, how he is pleased with what you have accomplished in your lives as individuals and as a couple.

A 40-DAY JOURNEY OF PRAYER FOR YOUR MARRIAGE

Prayer for Day 35

Free to Choose

Father,

Everyone has temptations for indulgence, whether food, drink, activity, or substances that can destroy our personal worlds, like alcohol and drugs. Realizing none of us are immune from painful addictions, free us to choose what is good tasting and enjoyable, but with moderation. Guard the internal set points of our desires so that we stop when we have had enough.

Through Jesus, our strength,
Amen!

"Man shall not live by bread alone." Matthew 4:4

Day 35 Reflection

Practice moderation today. Say *no* to a second cup of coffee or wine. Fast over lunch. Give up desert after dinner. Get up thirty minutes earlier than usual. Watch an hour less of television. Spend less time on your phone. Refrain from social media for a day. Then notice how it affects you. You may learn the source of your potential addictions.

A 40-DAY JOURNEY OF PRAYER FOR YOUR MARRIAGE

PRAYER FOR DAY 36

Grace to Accept

Father,

Today we bring before you the one thing we have been unable to accept in our lives. For us, it is _____. Even bringing it up causes us pain as we cannot seem to find a way to accept it. We don't understand why we can't change it or resolve it, nor do we understand why you have not answered our requests. Yet, we ask you now for more grace to wait in contentment and hope.

Through Jesus, who brings ultimate healing,
Amen!

> *"My grace is sufficient for you, for my power is made perfect in weakness."* 2 Corinthians 12:9

Day 36 Reflection

When we are hurting, frustrated, disappointed, scared or experiencing any other painful condition, the best antidote is openness and expression. Enter into a conversation with your spouse about your feelings around whatever you put in that blank today in the prayer.

Prayer for Day 37

Thank You

Father,

We have been spoiled by your lovingkindness. Even a brief glance around us right now exposes us to so many gifts from your hand. A spirit of gratitude is what we ask of you this day. Remind us to say "thank you" for the constant ways you care for us. Forgive us when we become greedy for more, when we covet the things of our neighbors and friends, when we grumble in childish selfishness. Thank you, Jesus, for all you have given us!

Through Jesus, the giver of all good things,
Amen!

"Overflowing with gratitude." Colossians 2:7

A 40-DAY JOURNEY OF PRAYER FOR YOUR MARRIAGE

Day 37 Reflection

Set the timer on your phone for 60 seconds. Then take turns finishing the following statement as many times as you can.

"I am thankful for..."

A 40-DAY JOURNEY OF PRAYER FOR YOUR MARRIAGE

PRAYER FOR DAY 38

Teach Us to Love More

Father,

It was love that brought us together as a couple and that love has sustained us through the hard times of our marriage. Do not permit us to take that love for granted or allow it to wither and die. Teach us to love more, to care with greater sincerity, to cherish more deeply, and to search for new and even better ways to say to this one who is my covenant partner for life, ***"I love you!"***

Through Jesus, the fountain of love,
Amen!

"Love never gives up." 1 Corinthians 13:7

Day 38 Reflection

Find a new way to express your love to your spouse today. Be as thoughtful and creative as possible as you come up with your own language to say, *"I love you!"*

A 40-DAY JOURNEY OF PRAYER FOR YOUR MARRIAGE

PRAYER FOR DAY 39

Forgive Us, Lord!

Father,

We all have a tendency to wander into **the far-off country of the prodigal.** For the times and ways we are still wandering, heighten our spiritual ears to hear your siren call that beckons us come home. And for all the reckless spending of your inheritance, we ask you to forgive us, Lord. Give us the eyes to see you running down the road with love abandon, ring and robe in hand, ready to have us return to your home and eat at your table.

Through Jesus, our brother who paid a debt we could never pay,
Amen!

> *"But while he was still in the distance, his father saw him and was filled with compassion. He ran to his son, embraced him, and kissed him."* Luke 15:20

Day 39 Reflection

Where is your *far-off country*, that place or habit or behavior that lures you away from the Father's home? Say the words of the prodigal son and watch as the Lord of heaven and earth drops everything to run to you, embrace you, kiss you, and welcome you home!

A 40-DAY JOURNEY OF PRAYER FOR YOUR MARRIAGE

Prayer for Day 40

Your Will Be Done!

Father,

This is the most challenging prayer of all—to surrender ourselves to your will and allow you to lead us in our lives, in our marriage. We are self-centered, wanting what we want, and we will need your grace to carry this out. Yet, here and now, we pledge ourselves to you. We give up our desires in exchange for yours. We ask from the depth of our souls, let your will be done in our relationship. Take us wherever you desire to lead, and we will follow you in complete trust!

Through Jesus, the Pioneer of our faith,
Amen!

"Trust in the Lord forever." Isaiah 26:4

Day 40 Reflection

Now it's your turn to compose your own prayer. What is left that you have not asked? What confession still needs to be offered him? What gratitude seeks expression? Write it out here and take it to him on your knees.

_____
_____
_____
_____
_____
_____
_____
_____
_____
_____
_____
_____
_____
_____

A 40-DAY JOURNEY OF PRAYER FOR YOUR MARRIAGE

ONE FINAL PRAYER

Self-Dedication to Jesus Christ

This prayer has been attributed to Ignatius of Loyola (1491-1556). It is one of my favorite prayers, but one I find so humbling. The sentiment of the prayer is the longing of my heart, though not always the reality of my life. It is how I close my time of worship around the Holy Table of our Lord.

Lord, take all my freedom. Accept my memory, my understanding, and my will. You have given me all that I have or hold dear. I return it to you, that it may be governed by your will. Give me only your grace and the gift of loving you, and I will be rich enough; I will ask for nothing more. Amen.

A 40-DAY JOURNEY OF PRAYER FOR YOUR MARRIAGE

I do hope you have found the last 40 days of praying these prayers to be a blessed journey for your marriage. As a Licensed Marriage and Family Therapist who has seen more than my share of pain and struggle from the couples who have given me the privilege of entering their lives, I can truly say with all my heart, soul and mind that the single, most important practice that will make the greatest difference in your marriage is to pray together. So, I leave you with this challenge—do not close your eyes to sleep until you have reached across the sheets, approached your spouse before you crawl into bed or even picked up the phone to call—and said a prayer together. It doesn't need to be long, articulate, wordy, or theologically profound. Just use your own words and say it, tell God what is on your heart and do it every day!

- Dr. Timothy Heck

A 40-DAY JOURNEY OF PRAYER FOR YOUR MARRIAGE

Dr. Timothy Heck

Dr. Timothy Heck is a Licensed Marriage and Family Therapist in Indianapolis, Indiana. He and his wife, Margie, are available for speaking engagements, including talks, workshops, lectures and retreats. You can learn more about his work and their ministry by visiting:

Liturgies.org

Contact: info@liturgies.org

www.ingramcontent.com/pod-product-compliance
Lightning Source LLC
Chambersburg PA
CBHW051408290426
44108CB00015B/2195